BETTER LIVING THROUGH POETRY:
A LYRICAL AUTOBIOGRAPHY

David L. Coulter, M.D.
Associate Professor of Neurology
Faculty Associate in Bioethics
Harvard Medical School
Senior Staff Neurologist
Boston Children's Hospital

1

Dedication

This collection of poems is dedicated to my family. My parents (Malcolm R. Coulter and Helena Urzendowska) knew I was different but did not seem to mind. I think my father recognized something of himself in me. My siblings (Malcolm A. Coulter, Dolores M. Coulter, Sister Theresa Coulter, IHM, and Melissa A. Scharrer) and I supported each other all throughout our life journeys. I was of course the middle child, which may explain a lot.

Most of all I thank my wife, Dr. Mary C. Cerreto, who was the first to see my poems when we became engaged 36 years ago. She has supported me ever since. Living well through poetry happens when we have the love and support of friends and family. I have had that love and support and am grateful for it. These poems would not be possible without it.

Acknowledgments

The poems "River Ballad," "Blasted Hopes and Wasted Dreams" and the series titled, "On Turning Seventy" were first published in the <u>American Journal of Geriatric Psychiatry</u> and are reprinted here with permission.

I would also like to acknowledge all of the poets whose works I read over the course of my life. Their works fill several shelves in my library. They were truly the "friends of my youth and guides as I grew" (as I wrote in the final poem in this collection). Perhaps this book will serve a similar purpose and be useful to someone else. That is really all I can hope for.

Comments On My Craft

I am an architect of ideas
Choosing words like bricks,
Care taken that they match
And frame a pleasing symmetry.

It grows by bricks in rows,
Truths simply stated
And easily overlooked,
Thought underpinning thought
And mortared by a dream---

Standing now complete,
A statement of my art.

TABLE OF CONTENTS

Introduction

When I was 13 years old and in the eighth grade, I would come home from school and curl up with a worn-out paperback copy of Emerson's essays that I had bought second-hand at a book fair for ten cents. His essay on self-reliance may have had the greatest impact on me. That same year I spent all of my money (six dollars) to buy a copy of the complete works of William Shakespeare, which I read one act per day so that I could savor his language. I started writing poetry around that time but mostly kept it to myself, burying my poems in notebooks and not sharing them with anybody else. Poetry for me, at that stage of my life, was a solitary pursuit. The poems in this autobiography thus begin with that awakening of my mind at age 13.

When I was 19 years old I started a practice of self-reflection that I have maintained throughout my life. Every year on my birthday I set aside some time for meditation about whether my life was on track and whether I was still pursuing my heart's desire. My college professor at the University of Notre Dame, Rev. John S. Dunne, described the "heart's desire" as "that place deep within a person where God's will and a person's own will are one." My annual birthday goal was to make sure my life was still in that place. Many of the poems in this collection were written on those birthday occasions, which is why I consider them to be the milestones of my life. This annual birthday practice helped me to avoid doing things that were not consistent with my heart's desire, to forego the seductions of success, and to focus on doing what makes life meaningful.

This collection pulls together all of the birthday poems I wrote during my life and includes other poems related to those themes. Part One, "A Young Man's Turmoil," includes the poems I wrote from the time I was 13 years old, a teenager just beginning to try to understand the meaning of life, to the time when I was 31 years old, no longer young but still trying to understand how to live well. The teenage poems are as immature as I was at the time. Some are playful, some are deadly serious, and some suggest what might come later. The young adult poems reflect my struggle to find my place in the world. Becoming a doctor meant that I relinquished the pleasures of my

20s, perhaps what could have been the best years of my young life, in order to pursue my heart's desire. These poems reflect that balance between vocation and vacation, between doing what I loved and knowing what I had lost.

   Part Two, "Living and Loving," presents poems that describe the challenges of my middle adult years (31 to 45) and demonstrate a mature eagerness for love. This sequence culminates in my courtship, engagement and marriage to my wife when I was 35. I have also included in this Part a number of poems about love and friendship which are relevant to that stage of my life. The "Celebration of Friends" is just that, my thanks to many of those whose lives intersected with and enriched my own during those years. "The Primer of Love" is an extended poetic exploration that has at least three interwoven metaphors. Like Joyce's "Ulysses," all of the action takes place during a single day. At one level it is a story about camping and canoeing in the wilderness of Quebec. At another level, each section explores a different aspect of physical love. And ultimately the poem seeks to understand the spirituality of love. The next poem, "Junction," is an attempt to tell a similar story through the minds of several characters, using narrative instead of metaphor to explore the physical and spiritual aspects of love.

   I was consumed by the demands of my career for the next 15 years and did not write much poetry until I was sixty. Thus the final group of poems included in Part Three, Harvest Time, deals with the challenges of getting older. It is a startling thing to wake up one morning and realize that you are now sixty years old. Where did the years go? And more importantly, what lies ahead? As I reached the culmination and fullness of my vocation in life and the end of my professional career, I realized it was time to focus on the mindfulness that I had hidden away for so long. I retrieved all of the old poems, wrote new poems, and determined to share them with whomever is interested. This book is the result. I am here now because I have lived my life through poetry, for better (as the title suggests) or for worse.

All in all, the collection represents a lifelong poetic narrative of self-reflection that I have pursued from youth to old age. It is thus an autobiography of mindfulness about what being a human being has

8

meant to me during my lifetime. The poem that closes this collection was written in Dublin, Ireland when I was 71 years old. I hope the narrative will continue for a while longer.

The title of this collection refers to the DuPont Company's old slogan, "Better living through chemistry." I'll put my faith in poetry instead.

PART ONE:
A YOUNG MAN'S TURMOIL

Reading Shakespeare (Age 13)

"Neither a borrower nor a lender be,"

Shakespeare says, so we must agree

That he who borrows is certainly

Not dependent financially,

Or as an alternative, probably

Has a soft heart or loose money.

My Personal Thanatopsis:
A Meditation On Death (Age 15)

The waters of life run but slowly;
On the bottom live the lowly.

But those who serve Him as they should
And live not only as they would

Find they stay not long in depths
But rise to the surface and are kept

In perpetual life and permanent mirth
Because they lived a life of worth

And heeded not the call of sin,
But lived their lives as worthy men,

And there they live in afterlife
Free from every petty strife.

So live not in sin, and sink beneath,
But live in God, in joy be wreathed.

To A Broken Phonograph

Lost!

Lost to my ears the strains of Brahms,
lost, too, the chords of the Trio,

Lost is the beat of December's friends,

Lost is the singing of swing!

Accustomed I was to all of the varied sounds

Of all of music's varied forms;

Yet no longer pulsate in my ears, alas,

Encompassing lyrical passions.

Stifled! (not silenced), they yet exist,

Exist in the depths of mind.

But oral formulation, severely missed,

(Someday restored?) is past---

Alas!

This poem, written when I was 16, shows that I could still have fun
with poetry when I was in high school.

The Death Of Abysoras

There is no life here. Once there was,
Until the enemy came like the devil
And wreaked destruction as Satan does---
Where once was a city, now is level.

No life remains in Abysoras,
For as the wolf attacks the fold,
So came Gom, with its death-dealing chorus,
Destroying all in the city of gold.

Gold can pervert man, but not subvert man,
As the Shezzar Fariz discovered that day
When the bloody avengers, soldiers of Gom,
Left Abysoras bleeding by the bay.

A new city rises where the old had been,
Not a city of gold, but a city of men.

The poem was written October 11, 1964, when I was 17. I have no
idea what this poem is about. It may be my attempt to reimagine
Shelley's "Ozymandias." Beyond that, I am clueless, all these years
later.

Inscription To A Friend

You all knew him. He was the one
First to laugh and first in fun,
Fun for everyone he knew,
Loyal, faithful, ever true,
Never slack'ning his faith and love
For Him who guides us from above.
To live for others—that was his code,
But now he walks the endless road.
Did I say endless? Never be;
On earth so friendly, yet so free,
He only yielded to enemy power
When had come the fateful hour.
Always he was the only one
To think in terms of others' fun;
He ne'er had thought of his own self,
But now he lies on France's shelf.

He gave his life so I'd be free---
Spared my life, but he made me
Ever bondsman to his lasting love,
The man, or boy, who ne'er had thought of
Aught but another. Now lies he there,

Having done more than his share.
I know that even as a boy
He gave his life to other's joy;
Friend of mine he was, I say
But how deserved I e'er to stay
In the friendship of another
Who'd treat me better than a brother
Who, dying, gave his life for me;
Thinking of others, thus died he.

Ennobled by all I hold most dear,
He turned his own, most virtuous ear
That ne'er had heard his spoken sin,
Eyes that ne'er had seen him cringe,
Mind that ne'er had been known to falter,
Thus laying his life upon God's altar,
Interposed his virtuous blood
Betwixt myself and the enemy flood.
Thus confused, the deadly blade
Struck him down, and as it made
Me ever mindful of his love,
His soul ascended to rest above.

This friend, this dear beloved boy,
Whose sole existence gave me joy,

Whose living life, from day to day,

So helped me live I ne'er could pay

The debt of love I'd always owe,

No matter where we'd ever go!

His body, ennobled by his selflessness

Now lies amongst the bloody mess

Men call a battle. What a name

To dress up valor, love and fame!

To mask all the but little things---

The acts of courage it always brings.

His body lies beneath the sand;

We tried to return him to the land

He loved so dear and fought to free,

And as he fought, he saved me.

What, and how, to e'er repay

A debt that grows from day to day,

That, even as I lie awake,

Thunders back to make me shake:

To return my share I'll always try

Somehow, someway, 'till I die.

Of course, I tried. I soon went back

To find his body, checked every crack,

Every scrap I could have used,

But came back with more love infused.

So gentle, kind, he thought of me;

Selfless virtue made his entry

Into my life, when his selfless acts

Brought me to renew God's pacts.

The life he lived was flawless, pure,

Sin he never could endure.

Living thus, he died, and rose to God.

They said of him that he was odd,

And that his virtue was a vice.

He cared not, loved all, wrong and right,

Loved me, even saved my life.

The poem is an attempt to imagine what young men might experience during wartime. At that time my main reference would have been World War II, so I think that is the dominant image in the poem (the landing at Normandy in particular). The poem was written in 1964 when I was 17, so I certainly was aware of the escalating war in Vietnam and the possibility that I would be drafted to serve there.

Bob Sutherland's Poem

Somnambulistically it flew,

As great tidings often do,

But no! Such was not to be!

Bad news! Death! A tragedy!

My beloved grandfather lives no more,

On earth he fulfilled his Godly chore;

He left behind an inspiration:

Love of people, God, and nation.

I know he lives, not here, but there,

In God's heavenly domain. To care

About him? Why should I then?

He lives in a heaven of honest men.

This poem was written in 1965 for Bob Sutherland, a good friend of mine who had been asked to write a poem for English class and was struggling with the assignment. We were both 17. Bob was a good person and a good friend, so I offered to help. I said, "Bob, what is important to you now?" He said, "My grandfather just died." So I wrote this poem for him in the morning before homeroom while we sat in the cafeteria. He said later that he got an A and the teacher said, "I never knew you had such talent." Good for you, Bob. You were a great guy and I was glad to help you out.

On Turning Nineteen

What can I say?
The world is full of people
   Who struggle for life but do not live.
But others, truly living,
Conscious of self and others,
   Twice resplendent,
For these I am grateful,
For these I rejoice,
For these live as men.

The only relevant truth is truth to life.
Who hurts no one and helps someone
Can never be wrong.

II.

To speak and say nothing is foolish: abjure it.
Not to speak, to say nothing, is wise: do this.
To speak and say something good:
This is for the best of men.
Follow them.

On Turning Twenty

My youth was old when this day came
And, closing out a score of years,
Turned around from a troubled age,
Admitting troubles that have not gone.

My body bears my youth untamed,
But not my thought, where age appears
And seeks dominion through constant rage
Over the master of the self-spent dawn.

On Turning Twenty-One

In a lonely room at dawn, silent,
Staring blank-eyed out the window
At a clear day in morning rising
On a sleeping street, impregnable,
Forgotten houses on a road to nowhere:
Lifting my eyes, I fall back on the bed.

    The times cry out for a poet

Dawn on New York rose like this,
Deeper, seeing over fields and hills
Sights sufficient for a bitter day.
And Hoosier farmlands have possessed me,
Their calm mornings a soothing balm
To my longings and fear and discontent.

    If I could be that poet

To be a million miles away,
A revolutionary, caught in a force
No land of sheep and silent streets
Can tolerate, but must destroy!
Lying quietly now is hell:
I shall not merely dream forever.

    Poetry is a chase after wind

Running Wild And Engaged

(Age 21)

Like the wild stallion---
   Rearing, kicking to strength's exhaustion,
   Muscles rippling in dynamic harmony, to defend his own---
Like this lone one, not lonesome
   (Having himself, his people, needing none else)
Like this fearsome, faithful patriarch,

I spurn your yellow hell of compulsive need!
Am not consoled by the sight of sheep!

Alone, in obscure and searing compassion,
I go forth---
   Lash out secured, and
   Rage against intrusion,
Jealous to death of what I am and am.

1968

"I'm white and I'm ashamed"---but no one cares,
No one comforts the suffering around them;
Morals are luxuries, things of the past,
Survival as a way of life suffices.

The man who wants to understand is pushed aside:
"Only a fool does not covet money!"
Inquisited, they have no need for an inquisitor.
But is it so much, then, to become a man?

I speak---and no one listens to me.
And when I listen, I wish I had not spoken.
It is the blind who wants to lead the blind!
"Life is not a walk across a field."

The poem was written 12-10-1968, when I was 21 years old. The last
line is taken from the poem "Hamlet" by Boris Pasternak.

Richland Balsam Mountain

Alone one possessed of newfound worth,
Vacation pursuing relentlessly, found
In mountains in time as old as the earth
Of space and time his personal ground.

Summit clothed in Canadian wood
Of spruce and fir and ground growth rich,
On Richland Balsam Mountain stood
One contemplating this new niche:

Forests of Oregon larch recalled
And happiness found in Verendrye,
In the rain on this peak of a southern bald
Where and what he had been, was, would be---

Vacation crowned in a new relation
Of timelessness, time and destination.

The poem is dated September 26, 1973. I had just turned 26 years old. "Newfound worth" refers to the fact that I had been a doctor for a little more than three months at the time the poem was written.

Bare-Chested In Mid-January

Sunlight plunging through the evergreen
In prison shadows blinds me willingly
This warm day, mid-January, as
A quiet in the air hangs lightly today.

I am called from winter's labors hence
Out to the forest and dull-green fields
Where now, all but naked, sport
Youth like I have lately been,

In study's respite chests bared, free
To the warming welcome of unseason sun.
This winter witness of magic in muscles
Lean, confinement-pale and soft,

A vigor rooted deep in the earth today,
Within gives flesh to shared desire
For freedom from self-bondage, longing
Towards day's sun's warm baring caring.

_____

I was 26 years old, a pediatric intern, and wondering where my youth
went.

The Bank Vault

You said it, you crazy woman,
You said it like a bank robber:
Just like compound interest,
The more you put in, the more you get out,
And you kept on depositing.
But you didn't count on my armor
O the policeman at the door.
I am the vault.
You never got beyond the teller.

I eat lives.
I search for them,
Seek them where they live,
And lock them away inside me.
I have never been robbed.

I have seen in other people's flesh
What I wanted to be, and eaten it;
I have taken their loving,
But I could not digest it.
I have received the love of those I have loved
And chewed it like cud,
Alone, inside, locked for the night.

You, my friends who love me,
I am rich from your interest.
But the door is unlocked now,
And I think I have turned off the alarm.
My gold is for the taking.

The poem was written when I was almost 27 years old and looking forward to life.

Zeffirelli's "Romeo and Juliet"

Time is running out on me.
More than twenty-eight years have passed
Since first my hesitant voice was heard.
But now my youth is old, grown cold,
And yet I live anticipating,
Lured by dreams of better times.
The time has come to sing out loud.

Better than that youth should be
And die before maturity---
Better than to die in youth
Though having loved eternally---
Is lifelong youthful wonderment
At beauty seized uncritically.

My time is running out to see.

The poem was inspired by the movie, but also reflects my own
concern about the passage of time.

On Turning Twenty-Nine,
After Hearing The Symphony At Meadowbrook

Today begins my thirtieth year under heaven;
I would not gladly be aught else
Than what I am, though often wish
Things said unsaid and undone done,
What never was now ever cancelled,
Already becoming determined to be.

I do not stray, still striving to excel;
The outcome of the past now present
And prologue to its consequence
Is what I am, by which I am,
Ready to take what there is to take,
And doing well what there is to do.

29

The Author As Voyeur

It is time I face this squarely,
Stop saying what should be is so
And things aren't what they seem.

I hear my teacher, old Walt Whitman,
Graft my chorus to his song,
And seldom stray from body-thoughts.

Lacking Walt's sure certainty
Celebrating men and women,
Buried accusations rise:

Pleasure seen in well-formed men
Becomes imperfect in my longing
Not to have so much as be one;

Women's beauty's faulted joy
Taunts my timid melody
With haunting dreams of what should be.

Perceiving my perceiving eye
I judge it impropriety,
Finding myself sexual guilty:

I look at bodies secretly,
Seeing what I want to be,
Knowing what should be is me.

On Turning Thirty
I. Letter to Myself

Are you afraid of turning thirty?
Look at yourself, you fearful fool.
Yes, you were a high school athlete
And yes, you're in your best condition
Since the year you turned eighteen,
But beautiful you never were
(Dreams of youth are always dreams).

What is there in adolescence?
These stumbling, half-grown boys you see
With half-formed struggling childish thoughts
Are not even what you used to be.
Twelve full years of living well
Have passed since you saw eighteen years
And make you what you are today.
Conscience is the tally of the years.

So fill your pipe, old man, and light it,
Think about the years ahead
And reconcile yourself to age.

II. The Skunk

The smell of failure haunts me
Like a dead skunk lying on the road,
Blotted out but not forgotten;
A poorly-knit parcel of vain endeavors
Striving to do just one thing well,
I live in ignorance of its name,
Like the skunk on the highway, miles away,
Oppressive although vaguely perceived.

What have thirty years of living brought
But few good friends and loneliness?
I am rent by many strings,
So many things I have to do.
My hopes are bathed in skunk perfume
That mocks and taunts me to despair,
And here in the study of my career
I am fenced in, overwhelmed by doubt.

The skunk, the skunk encircles me.

III. The Vishnu Schist

Time is the measure of human life,
Mortality ciphered against the eternal,
Easier to think about than God.
Like an athlete, in the morning
I descended into the Grand Canyon,
Ran past rocks, each older than the last,
Down to the depth of the inner gorge,
Surrounded by the sheer black walls
Exposed by the river-child Colorado,
Bathing my feet in its muddy water,
Palpable proof of the passage of time.

On the bank a stranger sat
Blond and tanned from many trails;
We spoke of time and life on earth.
"Do you feel like thirty?" he inquired.
I looked at my body and the ancient rocks
And smiled. "I feel about eighteen."
"Then rest and be content," he said,
"Look forward to a lifetime of adventure.
Your body is only as old as you feel."

IV. Pilgrimage to Zion

Such a sleep I had tonight!
My guilt-wracked body borne to rest
By the Virgin River's water
Lying gently at my side---
By this Virgin born in Zion.

Vain sorrows of my dying youth
I lay repentant at the Throne,
Whose pinkish stained white canyon walls,
Shining last night pale in starlight,
Stand like temples in the morning.

Ah, but I saw the hand of God
Thwarting all my vile temptations
In that sinful, neon city;
Fleeing to this wild abode
In search of Zion and forgiveness,
I found both in dreamless sleep.

Playing now at Taylor Creek
Or dancing in the wind at Kolob,
It is as if I am a child again,

No longer bound to a thoughtless past,
But borne into a brand-new childhood.

V. Letter to Saint Paul

("When I was a child, I spoke as a child,

I felt as a child, I thought as a child.

Now that I have become a man,

I have put away the things of a child."

Saint Paul, in 1 Cor. 13:11)

To Paul of Tarsus, prophet, teacher,

From a traveler, reconciled

And happy in this wilderness,

Comes this letter centuries late,

From places you have never been

To places I may never be:

Father and teacher, I have to say

The task you ask is impossible.

We had a feast to mark the day

Of mourning for the morning past,

Heretics at a wake for youth,

Recalling all that might have been

And dreams that will not come again.

Now we defy you, ancient one,

In your teaching to grow old,

And send our answer back to you:

Never again in innocence

Will be happy as a child---

But we still see, and will always be

In loving beauty young and free;

While there is breath and blood and strength,

What we were will guide us yet,

For we have lost the eyes of childhood,

Seeing now with childlike manhood.

On Turning Thirty-One

I climbed into the mountain's shadow
Sick to death for fear of time,
Desperate to reassemble
Fragments of my consciousness,
Recalling moments in my life
Experienced in wilderness,
In which I found solutions to
The jigsaw puzzle of my mind.

Effortlessly, answers come
When I am not pursued by thought
And time is lost, now free to see
And let the wild truth come to me;
Standing by the frozen lake,
I am prepared to join again
The world of living, confident
The picture will become complete
And what has passed will yet bear fruit.

For age is growth, not change, the years
Like roots, a strong foundation,
At every stage the younger phase
A source of everlasting youth.

PART TWO:
LIVING AND LOVING

The Yearning

Through all those years of isolation
Much was hoarded hardly used
That now decayed is almost lost;

Desperate to salvage something
From all of this that could reverse
These wasted years that hurtle by

(Which up to now have only led
To bars and instant assignations
Where strangers violate each other)

In nights of self-recrimination
At throwing sex and life away,
Guilty doubts inhibit sleep:

Each night lost is one less chance
To live and know the point of life
By loving like the way I dream.

Beyond the need (the constant yearning)
Beyond the search (the fruitless yearning)
Is only death and nothingness.

To Hell With All Your Prizes

To hell with all your fancy prizes,
The cold prizes that freeze the blood
With favors stiff as ice
And critical approval,
Prizes cold as death
That seal the lips of poets
Who dream of immortality.

My prizes are my pink slips
That show the world what fools
And ignoramuses editors are,
Who only know what sells
Or what their readers used to like.
My poems are hammers
That hit them on their heads
To wake them from their sleep,
The common sleep of common men.

Song Of The Open Road

Resting at an early station
On the road from apathy,
Restless wild imagination
Wanders into fantasy.

Mountains men have seldom seen,
Oceans I have yet to know,
Wilderness that fills my dreams
Are the places I must go.

Somewhere up the road is love
Tantalizing, out of sight,
Under a traveler's sky above
Raveling there in bright daylight.

Recollections of despair
And aimless days and nights of doubt
Dissolve like fog as I prepare
For love I cannot live without.

A Song Of Love

Love is a strange flower,
Blooming in the night,
Emboldened by the hour,
Withdrawing from the light.

What the lover sings
Knows nothing of the mind:
Beauty triumphant springs
From being entwined.

Love's flowers of the mind
Embrace the rooted flesh,
For in daylight they find
Sustenance afresh.

The Hope Of Love

The incandescent heat, that pain of love,
Without which life is nothing, bitter dross,
And poems but effort, that bright and searing flame
Must burn within me doubly fierce for loss.

So long forsaken, it may be past the time
Life gives a man? No misanthrope
Am I! No, a cautious man, unassured,
Who loving, could not love, but now has hope.

Emotion's watch alertly guards this path
It takes, this track of life so late prepared,
Desires that drive, reduced restraints of reason
Balance, seduction embracing those who cared.

For then the fallen fortress a palace seems,
And ivory tower becomes the bower of dreams.

Berkshire Nights

The western setting sun
Steals the light of day;
Dusky quiet mountains
Darkening with dread.

Daytime joys recede
As creeping foggy darkness
Emerges overwhelming
In the night-time of the mind.

Feelings of loneliness
Belong to the night.
Pain borne in daytime
Consumes the empty heart
That lies in bed alone.

Darkness needs a partner
To share the bed and blackness
And light the night with love.

Pathetique

From Sirius to Orion,
Cassiopeia to the Dipper,
Run a line to the North Star
And I'm in love.

The rain is gone.
I see her face in Polaris
Hung high over my house,
Leading me, pointing and
Shining on me.

Walk homeward, northward,
I'll never be alone again.

Sadly, this was wishful thinking, thus the title.

The Actor

All my life I've been an actor
Playing roles to get applause:
First I was a good little boy
Who always pleased his mother well
(But somehow never pleased himself),
And then I was a scholar cruising
Easily through years of school.

The whole world loved my acting job
But no one ever loved the actor,
Hiding from the audience
The hardest role of all to play
Because I could not play myself.

Every actor has his critics
To tell him how he played it wrong;
I gave myself my worst reviews.

But now I have a leading lady
Who lets me be myself with her,
Who loves me when I'm not on stage
And gives me all the strength I need;
I've never been off stage before.
She's such a loving Juliet
That I'm her perfect Romeo.

Parole

I know I've walked this street before
When I began my life of crime
Wanting what I could not have,

And it was on this evil street
I took the things I did not want
And lost the freedom of control.

But now I walk this street again
With cautious steps, a wiser man
Released from prison on parole,

Seeing all around me sins
That I could easily commit
By giving in to their temptation.

For who has not committed crimes
Against himself, then turned away
To start a new life on parole?

It's not like nothing happened, though
(The world still knows you were in prison
And every ex-con knows it, too.)

There is a person who believes
In what it is I want to be
And keeps me here redeemed and free,

The officer of my parole,
For whom I gladly turn away
From all the errors of my days.

The poem is an extended metaphor about adult relationships. The
idea of parole here is virtual, not real.

Engagement Song

I love the darkness of your hair,
The way you smile, the way you care
About the love we'll always share,
You are my one and only.

I wear your golden crafted ring
Because of all the love I bring
And give with every song I sing
To you, my one and only.

The love that makes my weakness strong
Is yours all day and all night long,
Together never going wrong
With you, my one and only.

Our matchless love no one can beat,
And so I pity those I meet
Who hope to find someone as sweet
As you, my one and only.

The pain of missing you will start
Whenever we must be apart,
For you possess my love and heart,
You are my one and only.

Wherever you are, there I will be,
For nothing means as much to me
As loving you eternally,
You are my one and only.

Prothalamion

This day God made for praising Him
We stand with you to celebrate
The knowledge of our love and joy

While we exchange our rings and vows
With words that represent commitment
Pledged today to live forever,

Grateful to receive God's love
For all His world and all mankind
Into the life we build together,

Having what we've never known
In happiness that now begins
With our communion here today,

Leaving now to share our joy,
Thanking friends and family
For all your love that keeps us strong.

The poem was written for my wife Mary Cerreto as part of the celebration of our wedding day. I turned 35 the next day and thus began the best part of my life.

The World Is Getting Away From Me
(Age 45)

The world is getting away from me.
I wake to worry about work,
Listen to the latest tragedies on the radio,
Then fill the day with suffering
Much of which I cannot help.
There is never enough time to write
The papers on which my career depends
And so I worry about that.
Home again, there are domestic needs
Like lawn and house and garden
And bills and budget to worry about.
And I need to read---if I have time.
Drained and exhausted, I go to bed.

There is so much more, so little time!
I haven't written a good poem in years,
Or read a good book, or even been to church.
How long has it been since I saw a mountain?
My life is going too fast,
I can't keep up with its demands.

I need to get off to the woods
To see things clearly again;
I need to slow my life down
So I can keep up with it.

A Celebration Of Friends

I. In The Wilderness

(For Joseph C.)

Clothed in armor like the sun
His lean and luminous body shone,
Expired a fragrance with his breath
I gathered in enchanted.

Encompassing arms of easy embrace,
When lost in despair, illumined
My hedged heart's own path
Homeward to himself---

And yet, like stolen treasure,
I held these jewels and did not have him.

But then a time of friendship came
And made us brothers of the light.

II. Adonis

Conquer thought, O my soul!
Astonish me with beauty,
Overpower me with love!

A beacon beauty springs
From out the world of things,
A sunrise, song or art,

And so do you, Adonis,
Fill these eyes with wonder
That drink your beauty now.

In a fine esthetic sense
The light of love's communion
Is shining in your eyes,

And dazzled by desire
I hesitate and falter;
To see you is enough.

III. Butterflies

As you sow, so shall you reap.
Looking out the open window
From a lonely double bed,
Moths buzzing at the porch light
Rob the night of sleep.
The one whose love I nurtured
Has not come home tonight.

   My love is somewhere,
   I don't know where,
   Searching for something
   I can share.

Butterflies come by instinct,
Careening out of darkness,
Enamored of the light;
I watch them flying closer, faster,
With a fatal frenzy
That ends with their incineration,
A love that has to die to be.
The night is strewn with bodies
Of those who sought that light.

   Come to me, butterfly,
   Out of the night,
   Fly not so freely
   Toward the light.

IV. My Friend Is Gone

Curtained windows closed again
Keep out the damp and chilly wind,
Allowing little morning light
This rainy day in early March;
The dark room lolls in somber peace,
A regained torpid solitude
Heavy in the stifled air,
Because my noisy friend is gone.

The lead weight lifted from my mind
Still hangs around my heavy heart
Remembering that storm of joy
Who burst into my loneliness,
Blowing like a warm south wind
That clears away congested fears
And cheers the wintry sadness there
With fragrance of a promised spring.

V. Circumference

(For Richard F.)

Old friend, are you laughing at me,
Sardonic smile a thousand miles
Captured in a Christmas card?

Once we had been high school friends
Sharing much unequally;
I saw my flaws responsible.

You went east and I went west
And changed (but never really changed),
Not quite the same boy I had been.

New friends took your place, old buddy,
I came to love for loving me
Who filled my mind forgetting you.

Ten years past and home again,
There is a void that has your name
My heart would like to fill with love.

VI. Friendship
(For Raymond R.)

Mute grief, that tore my fear-numbed soul, now go!
I have inquired, which answer this terror soothes:
The pain, that struck like numbing cold, I lose
As inquiry's fruit nourishes. Say not I know

What sorrow is; say, in my friend's trial I grow,
That that half my soul that is his (whom I accused
Of broken friendship) is by his suffering bruised
And battered, because he is. Such union shares our woe

And born of souls immortal, cannot be broken
While they live. Replacing grief is a desire
That, as once I prayed for him, to share some token
Of his mental pain, I might ease another fire

Consuming him. But some pain each alone must bear:
Whom I love, this, his suffering, I cannot share.

VII. Son of Responding Kisses

You gave me unforgetting kisses,
Haunting and responding kisses,
And with three kisses sealed our love.

One kiss said that you were glad
To share the night and dawn with me
While we took comfort in each other.

And one kiss said you knew I saw
Your manhood, looking in your eyes
As rich and dark as Mississippi.

When words had failed, your farewell kiss
Said somewhere, in another world
We could live in love forever.

My friend, when you have given all
To those who show no gratitude,
When you are weak, in need of strength,

Wrap your thoughts and arms around me,

Take refuge in responding kisses

And rest in the memory of our love.

I gave this poem to my friends David and John when they got married. The title and theme are based on a line from Walt Whitman's poem, "Vigil Strange I Kept One Night."

VIII. Woodbridge

A pattern of silken threads
Weblike woven between us,
In endless variation

Evanescent and strong,
In magic bonds of friendship
Binds us to each other.

Too weak to more than wonder
At the beauty of this work,
I live awestruck and amazed---

Pulled outward from myself,
I am tied to the world by a tether
Held tight to those I love.

The Primer Of Love

I.

Against a universe gray with fog
Merged with its watery gray reflection
On a motionless, still and fallow lake,
Our canoe moves slowly through the surface,
Untethered and hung in space,
Dipping paddles rippling the water.
We can see ahead only to each other,
Our vision spent looking for limitless shores.
Beyond the world of the canoe is nothing.

Returned from the chaos of a dreamless sleep
Beyond imagination, a world so gray
That nothing moved, we saw ourselves
And, turning about, saw next each other
Waking alongside in the tent this morning.
There began in camp then a reappreciation
Of sight and sound, touch, smell and taste
Like these bow-waves exploring water unseen.

Burnt by the early morning's August sunlight
The oppressive fog withers and slowly recedes.
Adrift in this lonely world floating past,
We kiss the shore against the void to one side
Hungrily seizing the sense of the other.
Moist as a newborn beast with foggy dew,
It is soon clear what sort of day this is:
We drift across the surface of a sky so blue
It is imperceptible from the water's edge,
And see as we look toward either shore
The perfect reflection of the land itself.
With a shirt removed in deference to sunlight,
Now mid-morning, the story of the day begins.

II.

Something is moving deep inside of me,
Beating out a melody, keeping time with my pulse.
It fills this bare breast to smothering,
Uneven, nearly taking my breath away,
Heaving chest harmonious in syncopation.
As it overcomes my heart with anarchy,
In proportion it gently quiets the mind,
Where it rests like a guest in the parlor
Or a visiting relative, come home.
I embrace the spirit that moves in things
Sharing memories of perceptions we have known,
Feeling like a member of a widespread family
And wondering if it is really I who comes home.

The clamor in my breast diminishes
As the conductor gets the orchestra in tune.
We run the canoe up on a sandbar to rest
And climb out stretching to lie flat on the sand,
Snuggling down onto its smooth, grainy bed.
I fondle the sight and the scent of these woods,
These streams, as surely as ever a lover did
The body of his beloved, caressed by them
And singing a song in tune with the universe.

III.

What could be better than swimming before lunch
On the beach of a sunlit lake in the woods,
Clothes aside and naked to the world?
Romping and splashing and swimming about
We play like children, though not as children
Do we appear exposed to each other.
A childlike touch, shoving and wrestling,
Meets full-grown flesh, now smooth and wet.
(I have not said if the day's companion
Be woman or man, nor will I say;
Let your imagination move on that.)

There is pleasure to be had in the vision here
Of the youthful body of either sex
And, touched by the feeling of the water and the woods
Singing inside of me, I drink it like wine
And dance intoxicated within my mind.
I know from this swimmer's touch exhilaration
Moves in my friend coordinate to my own
At being free and naked in this wild place.

IV.

Drifting swiftly down toward the rapids,
My body surges with anticipation
Of danger and excitement, thoughts still roaming,
Not yet harnessed to the adventure ahead.
Called from contemplation by the sounds
Of moving, falling, rock-opposed white water,
Arrived, we disembark to scout the route:
Shoot the current near the shore on the right
Then paddle midstream left of the fall,
Scrambling down the eddies to the pool below.

Crouched in the bow and squatting on my knees,
I have eyes only for rocks, known by their ripples,
Which riding upon would capsize the canoe,
And hear only the shouts of my companion
Exulting, instructing and changing our course.
The woods on the shore pass unperceived, a blur,
As we focus on each other and the water.
A slip, a wave, and we are thrown in,
The canoe driven past us near the bottom
To the pool we must swim to, riding the river.
Laughing, shouting, cursing, exuberant and happy,
And humbled by the wild, unconquered rapids,
Bodies aroused and enthralled, we quickly resolve
To carry back up and challenge the river again.

V.

In every act of love is coming and going,
A challenge made, an offer accepted gladly.
A melody heard stated in simple terms
Is good indeed and pleases; how much more lovely
To raise your voice and join in harmony,
Singing a song the world has never heard!
The song of this day is sung, reverberating
Back and forth, chorus and refrain,
By river and woods, companion and myself.

As plain to see as the trees across the lake
Is the dominion of wildness over my soul,
Building and shaping me, changing my heart
With love songs of rapids and gentle dreams.
By everything I love I am transformed
Acknowledging and accepting it,
Becoming that moment part of my beloved
In movements reciprocal, gifts of myself,
Changing my lover sharing my new-born heart.
I think these woods will never be the same
For the life we share with each other today
And will remember affectionately when I am gone.

VI.

Encamped in the tranquil late afternoon,
Enjoying the pleasure of the day at maturity
And sitting together, looking at the lake,
In silent seclusion our thoughts are conjoined
By love unspoken and the world around us.
A feeling rises, tingling within me,
From dark and hidden springs of sensation
To nourish me now, lengthened satisfaction
Strengthened and full at the peak of the day.
It is insistent, will not be contained,
Reaching out beyond my own perception
To find fulfillment shared with my companion
And companion feeling arising in my friend.
It is not enough to be in tune with the spirit
That moves wild things, as I have known it;
Love for the work of God must be shared.

VII.

What wound is mortal, under all the sun?
Turning about to encounter my weary colleague
Lying now beside me, partner today,
Evil said and done in mindless trespass
Of arguments and unkindness comes between
To shatter, pierce and paralyze the love I bear.
If there be death between us, all nature's spirit
Flowing through my soul must die as well.

Life is not a walk though quiet fields.
If love is goodness, hate is surely evil
That throws me back within myself,
Stills the melodious song of my days
And blinds my eye to the beauty of the world.
My hate-filled soul then moves as in a fog
To drift alone, never to be at peace
While there is evil in me for another.

Not by myself is hatred overcome
Nor can I clear a path for exploration,
But I must be in tune, within my soul
Encounter the spring of endless wilderness.
That which I celebrate, of which I am a part,
Joins me to nature, and so to nature's God
Breathing through creation, world and man
And living in my friend no less than I.

It gives me strength to go across in spirit
To heal the deathly wound through our forgiveness
And know another's heart as if my own.
And so we are united, not forming one being
But brought together in the being we share
By a spirit we find surrounding us
And living in all things---ours to know
By knowing what we are is in all things.

Junction

(A Story In Verse)

I. The Vision

Mark Mitchell lay on his back
Staring at a talcum-powder sky,
Sunlight burning on his breast
As sweat-smells of a simmering earth
Rose like steam, diaphanous in
A warm morning's light heat-haze.

He had run too fast this summer day
And as he stopped, surprising spasms
Of muscle-tingling, twitching giddiness
Commanded rest and new respect.

Like children picking wildflowers
In clearings shaded here, lit there,
Stealthy thoughts came into mind
As morning's heat on him bored deep,
Bathing him in pungent sweat.

Settling deep into the grass,
Insects crawled up over his arms
Chitinous and incongruous,
Exploring unresisting flesh.
Unlimbered unknown sensibilities
Were diffused to each nerve-ending,
The many recesses of body and mind.

In playful games of self-discovery,
Consensual with the field and sky,
Mark moved in a ragged rhythm
to the world and what was all about.

II. The Reality

The cracking sound of approaching steps
Recalled Mark from his reveries,
Ashamed of his passivity.
Unspoken silent obscenities
Restored him to himself, confused,
As he saw Dan, his dear companion.

A word about this Daniel Morgan.
Rain-swollen streams, alpine and glacial,
Were in his swift-flowing mind conjoined,
Moods rippling, breaking white-capped,
Swirling and bubbling unpredictably,
Joy smashed on hard-rock granite
Passing unseen deep, cold pools
That welled up incomplete, half-conscious.
The tensed edges of his careful speech
Kept aimless, brooding thoughts from awareness
As forces raged, caged within him,
Waiting for something to burst out free.

For resting, Danny gently rebuked
His friend, who received it with a smile
And thanked him for the past night's favor,
A ride to Kathy's house, his girlfriend.
Mark was loved, full freely loved,
And Danny smothered with that thought.

III. The Dream

Yes, Danny existed softly, if at all,
Having the pride but not the pleasure
Of silent secrecy and seclusion, safe
Within the edges of his razored thoughts
Hermetically sealed from life and death,
Longing for something, anything,
Unconscious, eternal, invigorating and unknown.

So in his mind he stripped, went swimming:
Bare bodies, naked beautiful bodies,
Life and strength in supple flexing
And soft, made loving to caress,
Soft, inviting, female and bare;
Blue water, sand tan, and skin flesh-colored,
Bare pale white deepening, mellowing,
Darker most bodies tantalizing,
Jewelry of a laughing eye---
Bodies dazzling kaleidoscopic
In laughter, love and fellowship.
A fugitive, fugitive and victim, Danny,
Stripping naked to enjoy the flesh!

Danny softened his face to smile
And taking leave of Mark, departed,
Seeking answers alone, suspicious,
Distrustful of desire itself.
He staked his entire hand on this:
That he could deliver from who he was
The loving man he wanted to be.

IV. The Love

Mark stood up, thought a moment,
Stretched, and set off down the road,
Running toward a rendezvous
With Kathy, his girlfriend, remembering
The time they shared, just yesterday.

Swimming at dawn in a pool of the creek
Where it flows past oak and hickory woods
Undergrown with saplings, thick with bushes,
The steaming of their stream-wet skin
Had joined the mists hazing day's sharp color,
Smoky fertile passions textured
In vapors of an orange-warm sun
Cool in the morning's rising above them.
Water creatures of a sensuous world,
All over awake, all clothes aside,
They had emerged and lain together
Laughing upward on the grass
At the blue sky's still dawn-pinkened clouds.

Swept by a flood-tide of emotion
And borne on the roaring, swelling bore,
He had ridden his reined-in, cresting desire,
Now floundering and foundering,
Now surfing boldly in control,
Exhilirated if not soon exhausted.
Passion's caps, hurled headlong
At the headland, white and frothing,
Struck the beach and withered to wash,
Riven by the rock-cliff's firm resistance.

There in the rock he recalled Danny Morgan
Carving his message, mute and eloquent
Testimony of his own adventures.
Reading his comrade's careful counsel, Mark
Strode lightly and determined down the beach.

They had savored together their great pleasure
And knowledge in this first exposure,
Saving future mysteries unknown---
And loved, and swam, and silently lay
Happy as never before or since,
Cool water bathing body and mind.

Mark ran on to his rendezvous
And that night, for the first time, drowned.

Note that for the purposes of this poem, the character of Danny
Morgan represents will and desire, while the character of Mark
Mitchell represents vulnerability and openness.

PART THREE:
HARVEST TIME

Wombsday

(On Turning Sixty)

It's nothing:
Yet, not unlike the rain last night
That lies in puddles on the pavement
And barely soaks the dog-walked grass
This early birthday morning, moist
With languid, humid, torpid silence.

But enough:
Still potent, passive, paralyzing
My thoughts and plans for the day,
The dawning decades, what's left of life,
All the things I could become,
Cancelled by what was and is.

And static:
Too late now for going back
To do the things I planned to do,
The daytime dreams dispersed again
By pallid, still and sunless air
That ticks the time away too slowly.

Yet something:

As sunset's colors darken earth

And clearing evening clouds unlock

The memories of what might have been,

Reminding me the setting sun

Will shine again another day.

So now:

As I look back, around, I see

The day is good if you wake up

And leave to memory all regret;

Let yesterday reveal today

And follow where tomorrow goes.

The poem is based on James Joyce's "Ulysses" which takes place during a single day, now called "Bloomsday." The title of my poem is a pun on that term and refers to the fact that I wrote it on my birthday.

Blasted Hopes And Wasted Dreams
(On Turning Sixty-One)

Stripling friends, four decades past,
School and team mates, play companions,
Imagined arms entwined again,

Conjured hither, rise! With reborn
Joyous hopes and boyish loves,
Think about what might have been.

Why did I survive, successful,
Writing down this lamentation,
You now ruined, lost, deceased---

You, with melted mind, now mad;
You, by greed laid low, in prison;
You, by tumor, untimely dead?

Fortune dealt a parlous hand, and
Justice cruelly cut the cards,
Making jokers of us all.

Better not to see our future,

Back when we were young and full of

Dreams the years would soon destroy.

Here with you in my remembrance,

Let us look at what transpired,

Reason searching for the reasons,

Finding none that satisfy: for

Providence may have loosed my luck, but

What that means I do not know.

Now I have to let you go and

Think no more upon the past, to

Focus on the times ahead,

Mindful that the meaning of it

Measures life by how one lives it,

Not by how the journey ends.

Lilacs And Roses
(On Turning Sixty-Three)

At first came lilacs, lavender lilacs,
So youthful and extravagant,
Their flowers fragrant in the spring:

While reaching for my heart's desire,
I thought I could inhale forever
And live with lilacs all my life.

But then came roses, blood-red roses,
In summer blooming, lovely roses,
Their sober stems with guarding thorns:

Now reaching for my heart's commitment,
I found a sweeter sustenance
Embracing roses in my life.

I planted lilacs on the left
And bushy roses on the right
Sides of my home, my heart:

Unable then, unwilling still
To choose between them, loving both,
I realized the road ahead.

As many as the ways to join
The lilacs and roses in our hearts,
So too are the ways to be fully alive:

And each of us, in our own time,
Will find commitment in desire
And joy in having what we love.

On A Day Like Today
(On Turning Sixty-Six)

On a day like today

The Swami sat in silence here
To think of healing, the rain not feeling,
In meditation by the river,
Young, at peace, not long to live
But living at this place forever.

Another day not like today

Underneath a river of ice
So many thousand years ago,
And long before this river flowed,
Pebbles scraping ancient rock
Carved the stripes I see today.

On other days just like today

My friends were born, and lived, and died
But never came to share this space,
This quiet place of peace and joy,
Nor sat with me, nor ever will
Except their souls be with me still.

On many days just like today

As seasons pass and years go by,
The river flows and insects fly,
While birds sing out and deer run free,
Around this place, unseen to me
Once present, now so far away.

But on this day of life today

My arms outstretched embrace the sky,
The woods and rocks, as all around
The world surrounds me where I stand
Or sit where Swami's peace abounds,
The universal prayer we share.

81

How blessed I am this day today

To be alive to celebrate
The gift of life this bounteous day
(A gift denied to friends who have died),
My gift to them the chance to play
And live again through me today.

On every day, not just today

I will be faithful, will not stray,
For some may walk these woods, not seeing,
But I will strive to see, not walking,
And simply pray, in my own way,
Like blessed Francis, all my days.

River Ballad

(On Turning Sixty-Eight)

I.

Torrential rain, a sudden summer squall,

Sends rivulets that soak the thirsty earth

And join in freshets towards a waterfall,

A nascent stream in new formed robust birth,

Each drop so rare and precious, multiplied

By every other drop that forms the course,

All surge together, impact magnified,

And swell the pond that is the river's source.

II.

The outlet of the rain-filled little pond

Grows larger as it drains the summer flood

And carries all the droplets far beyond

Their origin, free-flowing, like fresh blood

That vivifies the land and life downstream,

Becoming first a creek and then a river,

Its current amplified with youthful dreams

That challenge limits which its banks deliver.

III.

The river plunges, smashing past the rocks
And crashing on the rapids as it goes,
Then settles down, constrained by dams and locks
And folks content with how the river flows,

And yet, within the river, drops endure
That still recall the thunder of their birth,
But cannot slow the flow that time ensures
Will someday end the promise of their worth.

IV.

The river has matured, but still it carries,
In calm and fragrant currents that conceal
The snags and bars that threaten the unwary,
The risks no river forecast could reveal,

And still it bears the drops that bring new life
By irrigating fields along the plain,
Invigorating all with strength and rife
With fruitful growth that renews life again.

V.

But ah, the aging river, safely past
Those snares and dangers, all its duties done,
Meandering in peace throughout the vast
Inheritance its ancient valley won,

In loops and bends across the fertile land
It passes oxbow graves of what it was,
Toward the place no river can withstand,
Where nature cycles all that water does.

VI.

The drops that traveled to the river's end,
Where delta swampland stretches far and wide,
Born long ago in many storms, now send
Whatever was, is now and will abide

To meet the waiting, welcome, timeless sea
That will envelop all the river gives,
But yet they trust that their identity
For all eternity will somehow live.

VII.

These drops that came from thunder to the sea
Are all unique and special, yet as one
They have become what they will always be
Long after their great river trip is done,

But our life journey, glorious and grand,
Has no need now to end, today or ever,
Our final scene remaining yet unplanned,
With much to do between now and forever.

The Last Gathering
(For My Father-in-Law, Sebastian S. Cerreto)

The fading autumn rose, now brushed with snow,
Its green leaves pale but flowers still blood red,
With dignity and grace prepares to go
To glory in the endless years ahead.

And like that rose, our patriarch resolves
To gather one last time before he goes
His brood of chicks to him, as life dissolves
To legacies that bloom as their lives grow.

Through ninety years of trials, growth and joy
The father of us all has brought us through,
And so we praise what death cannot destroy
And pray, "God speed, our love and thanks to you."

Whenever we shall see a rose so red,
We shall recall with love the life he led.

On Turning Seventy

I. Living On Borrowed Time

Seventy is a nice round number,
Three score years and ten,
Quite enough for the Bible (1),
But not enough for me---
I want to keep on growing
And live on borrowed time.

Which raises a couple of questions:
From whom is my future borrowed,
And what are the terms and the rate?
How can I make the payments,
And when will the loan be due?
If I can't pay, who will?

If I borrow it from my ancestors,
Will my descendants have to pay?
Can I leave it to them as my legacy
For them to spend as they will?
What if I want to go back
And borrow a little more time---
Will good years still be there?

I owe no cock to Asclepius (2)

And hope to enjoy my time

Until the loans expire,

For what I need is simple,

When all my debts are paid:

To sit with friends at the campfire

Sharing a lifetime of stories

While smoldering embers fade.

---

1.   Psalm 90, verse 10: "The days of our lives are three score years and ten; and if by reason of strength they be four score years, their strength is but labor and sorrow, for it is soon cut off and we fly away."

2.   See Plato's Phaedo (the death of Socrates)

II. Whistling Past The Graveyard

Just walking here,
Stepping quickly now
Past the cemetery,
Looking straight ahead,
Avoiding thoughts and
Blocking fears,
Trying to whistle
A cheerful tune
And not see what is
Next to me.

This is not a happy poem.

Cemeteries scare me.
I respect and pray for the gentle repose
Of friends and family buried there,
Resting in their final reckoning,
Their silent graves a compelling vision
Of beckoning mortality,
Insistently reminding me
My time will come.

But cemeteries will not hold me.
I will not have a gravestone

Because there won't be any grave.
My molecules will survive recycled,
Nourishing the worms and fishes
Living in the lake forever.

I do not wish to go there easily
But fear my time might come too soon
Before I finish what I need to do—
So many poems still to write,
So much to give,
So much to share.

And what if that is all there is?
A lifeless body, no afterlife,
No glory hallelujah---
Nothing, nada, finis-kaput?
What then?
I need a visa, a promise of travel
To wherever it is I will finally go.

Maybe
(I am walking faster now)
If I can whistle loud enough
I will not hear
The waiting sounds of wailing
And the distant dirge of death.

So that's my plan.
I'll keep on walking
Past the graveyard, past the fear,
Walking and whistling and praying for time
To keep on going as long as I can,
Until I can't.

III. Hurtling Toward Eternity

While walking barefooted on the sunburned beach in Brewster
And cooling my feet in the flow of the freshwater creek
That furrows the sand on its path toward the sea,

I followed its current, recalling its youthful sources
Arising in mill ponds, then coursing past meadows and brambles
To end in the salt water now just a few feet away.

Still fearless and faithful, I resolved to again bathe my feet
In the vast Atlantic's inevitably rising tide,
By the full moon surging and soon submerging the beach,

And then retreated to the sand hills defying the sea,
To sit with reunified friends of my freshwater years
And watch the eternal ocean consume it all.

Not far from here a feckless humpback whale
(Perhaps the one we saw just yesterday)
With youthful vigor, beached itself and died,

While older whales continued on their way
To breed again, but they must wonder, too,
Why young ones die and older ones survive.

So here I sit barefooted, watching time
Relentlessly flowing like the waters of Paine's creek
As days and years pass all too quickly by,

Completely unprepared for what comes next,
More old than young, my pilgrim soul exposed,
With life still patient but impatient with myself,

And see that all of the things I would still like to do
Come down to this: to surf the rising tide
Until it turns and washes me away.

DUBLIN, 2018

I am different, like no other

Like Joyce, I walked St. Stephen's Green
In my guayabara shirt (1), easily seen,
And read Yeats' poem, "Easter 1916,"
His terrible beauty still changed utterly (2).

I crossed the Green and stood face to face
With Thomas Kettle's statue protecting this space
And silently read out loud to his ghost
His farewell poem to the child he loved most (3).

I am different, like no other

Maybe I am more like my Irish family
In love with this land and its poetry
Who rose up to fight for their liberty---
But actually I am not like them either, really.

I am most like the writers whose poems I knew,

Friends of my youth, guides as I grew,

Apostles of a self-reliant god out of view

Whom I worship when I to my own self am true.

---

1. A guayabera shirt is the typical shirt of Cuba, so to wear it was very much different from what one usually sees in Ireland.

2. Yeats' poem has the recurring line, "All changed, changed utterly: // A terrible beauty is born."

3. Kettle wrote his poem, "To My Daughter Betty, The Gift of God" four days before he died in battle in World War One. The final lines of the poem are inscribed on his statue in St. Stephen's Green:

I died not for flag, nor King, nor Emperor,

But for a dream, born in a herdsman's shed,

And for the secret Scripture of the poor.